MW01228646

Managing for Meteors

Preparing Local Government Leaders Before the Impact

Managing for Meteors

PREPARING LOCAL GOVERNMENT LEADERS BEFORE THE IMPACT

SHANE SILSBY

For Anne, Carson, and Gavin...

*And all of my career mentors,
colleagues, and partners...*

And my parents.

CONTENTS

PREFACE

After serving 20-plus years in government and holding various leadership positions at multiple agencies, I switched to the private sector and spent time in operational, strategic, and executive-level roles. As you might imagine, observing governments from the other side of the fence was revelatory. This shift marked a transition from a career almost entirely comprised of government service, which only added to my passion for and experience in building effective and efficient organizations.

After obtaining bachelor's and master's degrees in civil engineering, I stayed local in blue-collar Lansing, Michigan, working within a strong-mayor form of government supporting a community familiar to me. From there, I moved to Phoenix, Arizona, and experienced a new climate, literally and organizationally. Phoenix was the nation's largest government agency with a city manager leadership structure (and the 5th largest city). Eventually, my career path brought me to Orange County, California, and a journey with one of the largest and most complex local governments in the country (as the nation's 6th largest county). Then, private sector experience seemed to complete the panoramic view and provide further opportunities for improving communities through quality infrastructure and services and seeing what worked or what could be improved. One of the ways to assist with the implementation of these improvements is through the broader sharing of my applicable knowledge and understanding.

This book provides a conduit for passing on that experience, raising questions, and providing tools for new leaders to consider for enhancing the functions of local governments and getting prepared ahead of major disruptors.

\- Shane Silsby
www.silsby-sa.com
California, USA

INTRODUCTION

A t first glance, "Managing For Meteors" might seem like an odd title for a book to help government leaders navigate the maze of daily challenges and prepare for the unknown. But given recent history, the possibility of something flying through space directly at us might not seem so remote. The Internet of Things and mobile devices have revolutionized the way we communicate, work, learn, and entertain ourselves – including the ability to access information at the touch of a button and work from anywhere. The emergence of artificial intelligence technologies revolutionizing many aspects of our lives and has already led to self-driving cars, workerless manufacturing processes, and tools for medical diagnoses. Then came a global pandemic, the effects of which we are still discovering and attempting to mitigate.

That brings us to meteors. For leaders new to government or new to a leadership position, preparing for "meteors" should become a fixture in one's daily thought process.

So, what is a meteor? A (metaphoric) meteor, in any organization and especially in government, is this unavoidable thing that is coming at you. Whether foreseeable or unexpected, it's that object large enough to disrupt the operations of your organization. Meteors interrupt daily operations by consuming time and resources, almost always in an inefficient manner.

When meteors hit, you don't want to face them alone or try to develop mitigation plans in real-time. That is the core purpose of this book, to advise new leaders on multiple strategies to prepare for the meteors of the future by taking strategic actions today.

The primary keys are to have effective and efficient processes in place, operations ready, and teams aligned so that resources and strategies can be activated or adjusted to address that meteor. As with the meteors flying through space, these disruptors come in any imaginable size, shape, speed, or direction.

Examples of Meteors

- **Financial crisis**

  Aside from an event like the Great Recession of 2007-2009, a financial crisis could also occur at the local level, like a city or county bankruptcy, a loss of significant tax revenue, or an unanticipated major investment necessary to address an unsafe structure or an out-of-compliance computer system. It could result from the long-term consequences of poorly managed finances or deficient infrastructure maintenance.

U.S. Capitol Building - Washington, DC: New or revised federal laws can be a significant disruptor for local agencies.

- **Mass staff exodus or key leadership transition**

Impacts might not arise from within your specific work group, as it could be the departure of a key leader like a CEO, City Manager, or an elected official who took a lot of the momentum with them. It could also be the loss of a large number of key staff possessing critical knowledge or specialized skills.

- **A global pandemic**

After 2020, this example seems obvious, but most government agencies generally disregarded warnings of a global pandemic because it didn't seem to merit immediate prioritization of time and resources. Armed with hindsight, would your agency have liked to offer more virtual or remote options for providing services to your constituents in March 2020?

- **Natural Disasters**

A tornado, wildfire, hurricane, flood, or earthquake can shatter the operations and revenue base of a local government and can create countless urgent tasks. If the impacts of these events are prolonged, how will you deliver regular services to the community in parallel with mitigating the disaster?

- **A Major Federal or State Initiative**

This could come in the form of either a mandate or a funding surge, like the infrastructure funding acts recently passed by the U.S. Congress. The federal government responded to the pandemic with operational and infrastructure funding, similar to spending measures in the wake of the Great Recession, aimed at creating stability and improving infrastructure at all levels of government.

- **Rise of the gig economy**

This new economic model, in which people work for themselves often on a contract basis, is driven by the rise of the internet and mobile technology. These enhancements have made it easier for people to find and work with clients while reducing reliance on large corporations or governments to provide gainful employment. The gig economy is likely to continue growing, with implications for everything from employee attraction or retention to the provision of healthcare.

- **Meteors can be positive too…**

Even a meteor with positive intentions can create stress and additional expectations for you. More money for your department, moving to a new building, getting a motivated leader – all will have an impact.

It's really about the thing that is so disruptive that you cannot adequately address it AND maintain your regular course of business. Agencies need to be prepared in advance for these eventual meteors.

Many of the disruptive forces of the 21st Century have created knowledge and experience voids within almost all government agencies. These gaps have been further accelerated by the pandemic, the generational transitioning of the workforce (e.g., the Silver Tsunami), the lack of available applicable talent, and career shifts by many workers.

In some respects, the impacts of the global pandemic are similar to the Great Recession, when organizations were caught flat-footed and had to enact deep cuts and major organizational changes based on steeply declining revenue sources. Compounding these issues is the reality that governments cannot bounce back quickly to backfill positions frozen, eliminated, or vacated due to retirements or other attrition factors. Additionally, higher private sector salaries can quickly break a tie for those considering a role in public service.

The voids created by disruptive forces continue to create major challenges for government agencies. For example, the lack of understanding of new technologies has made it difficult for most agencies to develop and implement new programs and services that can take advantage of industry innovations. Limited expertise in new fields has also made it difficult for agencies to adequately address complex challenges, such as cybersecurity and climate change. The lack of trust from the public has made it difficult for agencies to get the cooperation they need from the people they serve or to raise taxes for needed infrastructure or services. These voids are making it problematic for agencies to effectively carry out their missions and are contributing to several challenges, such as ineffective regulations, poor decision-making, and a lack of focused accountability.

So, between the disruptive forces already in progress and the dynamics introduced by the pandemic, we have a great many new government leaders who might benefit from a little help and shared experiences.

This book is intended to provide a head start for new or newly promoted leaders in government, helping them avoid spending excess resources to research or trial strategies on ineffective initiatives, and to prepare their agencies for the eventual impact of meteors.

The Adverse Effects of Meteors

One significant adverse effect [and common among meteors] is the disruption of daily functions. Another is that these disruptions peel back the visible – or public facing – layer to reveal the true level of organizational preparedness. The ability to effectively respond to meteors affects the credibility of both government agencies and their leaders. Further, the rise of social media, and other forms of organic journalism, have made it easier for the public to hold

CityScape - Phoenix, AZ: At the time, this development represented the largest private investment in the downtown area.

government agencies accountable or to highlight particular issues in a way that may not be fair or deeply researched. The American people have a general distrust of government that has worsened in recent decades. One goal of this book is to equip leaders with strategies to rebuild trust in government by successfully navigating hardships and improving the efficiency and effectiveness of operational duties and constituent services. So, the meteor hits. Even if the event could not have been foreseen, your response is exposed to the light of public scrutiny. It's not fair, but the residents, visitors, and taxpayers believe that government agencies should have all the answers all the time. They also expect governments to be fully staffed and ready to adapt to any situation. Those are the constant expectations, especially from people who pay a heavy tax burden to those governments or the persons elected to represent those constituents. As the saying goes, this "perception is their reality."

When it matters most, people expect their governments to perform. This book was designed as a tool to help leaders get prepared to do exactly that. The following content is organized to address topics within government organizations, then transitions to dealing with external partners and the public. However, each chapter is written in a way that can be accessed as needed - like a toolbox to help new government leaders quickly read through strategies on key organizational topics.

1

PREPARING FOR "THE METEOR"

Decades of experience in municipal governments have brought a great many opportunities to launch projects, initiatives, and reforms. Those undertakings brought both highly successful results and opportunities for improvement. Through it all, every major effort has either taught lessons or reinforced timeless principles of effective leadership.

Managing for meteors means establishing a culture developed for success and instituting supporting policies, practices, and procedures to enhance preparedness. Beginning as the director of Orange County Public Works marked a memorable step along the career path of a journey from a Midwestern small town. The department had nearly a thousand positions and a seemingly endless supply of people offering their ideas or perspectives. Some ideas involved potential projects or operational initiatives while others were comments on the hope for a new and improved culture.

Perhaps the most important component of a successful

culture is the daily expectation of hard work. For many, including this author, the lesson of hard work was learned through athletics. Thankfully, the joy of high school sports was followed by the opportunity to play basketball at the college level for a couple of years. Athletics is the ultimate meritocracy, with results earned on the field or court. Less-talented teams can learn that they might defeat superior opponents by working hard and preparing diligently to execute their coach's strategies and tactics.

But executing strategies is only part of the work. A leader must also prepare organizations for meteors, those unexpected events that can impact results and define careers.

For new leaders, the effects of meteors can be compounded by the lack of insight that can be mitigated from the benefit of experienced advisors or mentors. This book was composed to serve as an advisory tool, helping leaders during their first time in government, a leadership role, or a key management position. The goal is to offer the benefits of twenty-plus years in government, enhanced through private sector experience, to help with navigation of unexpected issues or challenges and to offer foundational improvement strategies.

Most meteors have at least two common characteristics: 1.) a disruption to the way your organization functions; and 2.)the level of true preparedness is revealed. The ability to respond to these disruptions affects the credibility of the organization and the entire government agency.

Civic Space Park - Phoenix, AZ: This multi-agency project included a 4-story tall art exhibit and a historic building.

Changing culture to meet expectations

For a new or emerging leader, the first task is to understand that you are entering a state of transition. You need to make ready those key staffers, leaders, supervisory chain, elected officials, and legacy community leaders that the agency will be entering an organizational adjustment period. If people know and understand the "why" behind your efforts to improve or update the organization, they may be less likely to oppose recommended changes and may even become supporters.

Also, if you ask someone for their advice or insight, they may be more open to changing their position or perception, at least for that conversation. In addition to validating them as important, you may also be able to include them as investors in the organization's future success.

At the County of Orange, we collected information through employee engagement efforts on what was important to them in a few focused areas. The results were overlapped with industry trends and updated business practices. Then, those efforts were customized to that government agency and that geography, to meet the unique characteristics and expectations of the community.

Strategies were ultimately melded together to propose improvement initiatives through multiple actions. And then, after 50 plus meetings with key staff and with elected officials and leadership for the agency, we refined and rolled out a multi-step transition plan. Advance notice was given through various formats and multiple venues because change is difficult even if the intentions are well-meaning. This strategy has had frequent success and should be replicated every three to five years because of changes in people's priorities and perceptions and industry advancements.

Doing this correctly and showing evidence of directly linked survey responses with proposed initiatives from leaders can bring multiple benefits. This builds trust with your work groups by demonstrating that the responses will be read and potentially prompt responsive applicable actions. While that might not address every issue, it has partially changed the culture and heightened the investment of each employee in their respective role.

Two types of success

There are basically two types of success; one arises from maneuvering operations and the other comes from executing the implementation of capital resources. The successes coming from organizational or operational refinements tend to be soft wins, with potentially more subjectivity in the measurement.

In contrast, hard or objective successes may involve the delivery of bricks-and-mortar capital projects. Achieving a revenue initiative to offset annual taxes in your organization to render a more robust financial footing is a soft win. However, an animal care facility in Orange County, the first new regional one in 70-plus years, is a brick-and-mortar objective win.

Different types of success are often the result of varied strategies and types of experience. Reinventing the culture of an agency requires the zeal to achieve quick, soft victories and the patience to pursue long-term capital successes. After a day handling immediate issues, the late-night hours in the office or at home at the dining table might bring the only windows of time to work on the meteor mitigation planning and long-term projects or initiatives that can have legacy impacts.

Orange County Admin. Building - Santa Ana, CA: This mega project was the first major downtown investment in 30 years.

2

CULTURE AND CREDIBILITY

Triumphant and timely results will generate trust among leaders, colleagues, elected officials, and the public. The resulting effect can also improve navigating the bureaucracy to bring results with greater speed and efficiency. The personal or agency brand is based on trust and track records. Colleagues and leaders alike should believe they can depend on the performance, efficiency, and transparency of you and the agency.

The years have taught that one can never over-communicate, especially on the premier issues, for keeping staff focused and aligned. Transparency of information is crucial because its absence creates voids. Human nature being what it is, voids are filled with people's own perceptions or rumors or the topic of the day. Sadly, people may prefer to believe sensationalized gossip, even when an easily accessed truth lies elsewhere.

Transparency is important in both large and small organizations. However, in larger organizations with less direct in-person or on-site interactions, disseminating information quickly and accurately carries heightened importance.

Encouraging transparency might seem like routine common sense. However, it is one thing to cognitively understand the need for transparency, but an entirely different approach to include it as a highlighted priority when communicating among staff or between departments.

Transparency should become a habit, similar to muscle memory in throwing, shooting, or hitting a ball. Consistent awareness of transparency includes exercising it and making it an expected part of the new culture. Each employee desires to receive information when, how, and in quantities THEY prefer, and an ongoing focus on transparency can address these customized interests.

Advance, don't retreat

A previous executive role brought the opportunity to implement twice-a-year leadership summits called management "advances." Each year fall and spring offsite events were planned. The fall forum brought reflection on the previous year and goals for the coming year. The spring forum included concentrated efforts on new and ongoing initiatives.

Originally, these forums were called retreats, but a U.S. Army Corps of Engineers colonel and personal mentor provided meaningful insight into the title of these gatherings. He explained that we shouldn't be retreating as an organization; we should always be advancing. That might seem like a small detail, but when establishing and maintaining a culture, each small change becomes one piece in the mosaic of a re-envisioned organization.

These events included inviting all managers to the morning session for updates applicable to all business units and discussions about improvement or transparency initiatives. After that session and lunch, the higher-level leadership team stayed to refine the results of the morning's discussions and convert those ideas into actionable initiatives.

Special events of this type require an extra level of commitment and resources. It takes time and funding to secure a venue, use a facilitator, develop materials, and provide food - that was why they were only held twice a year. But that was the minimum cadence to keep the leadership engaged, acquire feedback from managers, and improve alignment on strategic goals.

Getting seemingly disparate groups to communicate is often quite challenging, which was why it was essential to get them offsite and at tables working together. This also provided the leadership team with opportunities to come and go from various conversations and learn about issues first-hand.

The management advance events included designated program tables, one for each functional service area.

Despite being co-workers, each participant was given a name badge. The badge displayed two seating assignment indicators, the first being the letter of the service-area table, e.g., the functional area or the group you work in daily. The second was a number that rotated each participant to a different table to inter-mix managers from across the organization. Each participant had two different arenas in which to listen, learn, and offer insight to the others. The topics, discussions, and group dynamics brought the type of variety that inspired meaningful ideas, which led to future initiatives or goals. These events can also create renewed energy to sustain long-reaching agency efforts or jump-start new objectives.

MANAGEMENT ADVANCE TABLE SEATING

25 attendee example

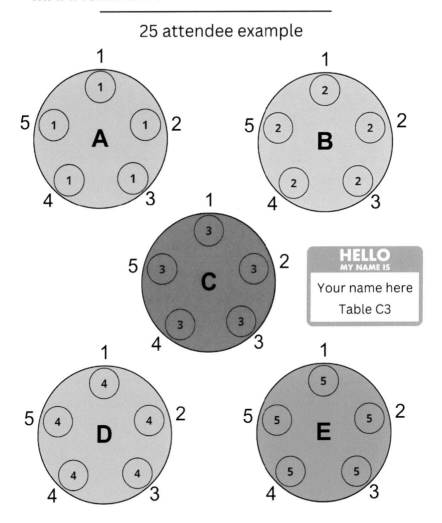

HELLO
MY NAME IS
Your name here
Table C3

Lettered tables = Functional or Department grouping (5 persons each)

(#) = Cross collaboration grouping

Hiring Practices

Few acts affect a culture more immediately and substantially than hiring practices. Logic dictates that the larger the organization, the more people one has to bring into the organization every year to mitigate vacancies. Regardless of your leadership successes, natural attrition occurs from people that retire, get different jobs, suffer from health issues, start new families, or move out of the geographic area.

Hiring choices and practices will establish a trend, either toward or away from improving agency culture. Accordingly, that is one of the areas where leaders, elected officials, department heads, and anyone involved in hiring need to be mindful.

Multiple studies have demonstrated that the number one reason why people leave their job is their supervisor. Unfortunately, supervisors can also be bad employees, but they can cause more damage because good employees will leave because of them. That's why it's especially important for government agencies to have good managers and supervisors, resulting from improved hiring practices.

So how does a leader make that happen? The most obvious answers are to establish consistent hiring practices, capable and non-biased selection panels, and thorough job descriptions. But there's more.

Standardizing position descriptions and the associated

recruitment information is one important tactic in the battle for filling vacant positions. When readying to hire one position, the creation of an updated standardized set of documents can then be utilized now and for future recruitments.

For filling multiple vacancies, these standardized documents can be accessed so that every job description is not customized. Standardized position classifications also provide a foundation for consistent recruitment information.

Another concept is filling multiple vacancies with single recruitment. Suppose an organization needs multiple new managers. The positions may be in different groups, but tweaking the recruitment information can allow posting within one-time period, with one high-level selection panel, resulting in the filling of multiple vacancies out of that single effort. The second component of this strategy is minimizing recruiting actions while maximizing the number of positions filled.

And then the third component is whether a leader focuses on hiring internally, externally, or both. Employees may often suggest hiring internally because that is perceived as better for morale.

Like many ideas, that concept is not as simple as it seems. Let's say an agency has a hundred vacant positions. Suppose each of those hundred vacancies is filled with internal staff through promotions or transfers. At the end of that process, how many vacancies does the agency have as a result of those actions? The answer, of course, is that 100 vacancies remain because of the promoted employees vacating their old positions. Much energy and resources were expended in this scenario, with no objective gains made to reduce vacancy numbers and provide new resources to address workloads.

No one was born in the department or agency. Every employee was hired externally at some point. If good candidates are not organically rising internally, the agency should emphasize workforce development, offer stretch assignments, and give employees ways to enhance their career portfolios.

In Orange County, the direction was to encourage staff to simply focus on hiring the most qualified candidates. At the end of a year evaluation period, reviewing the hiring actions revealed that the total number of resulting new hires was 150, with 75 hired internally and 75 hired externally. At first, it was surprising, but the outcome confirmed the validity of the approach to hiring the best available candidates.

Internal promotions keep continuity, minimize disruption, provide historical context, and stabilize morale by promoting high-performing employees.

External hires benefit an agency by bringing creative ideas, renewed energy, insight through fresh eyes, and additional resources to address workload demands.

Black Mountain Blvd. - Phoenix, AZ: Corridor project that included several neighborhood elements to enhance credibility.

3

STRUCTURE AND STRATEGIES

The first two chapters have examined ways to prepare for unexpected meteors by focusing on improving culture. That culture, refined through hiring practices, enhances credibility and fosters better communication with transparency. This shift in focus also helps colleagues become receptive to new ideas and projects and work with peers from other segments of the agency, to prepare for those inevitable meteors.

Beyond the culture of the organization lies its actual hierarchical structure. One of the lenses through which to view the efficiencies of structures is Parkinson's Law, a landmark theory for understanding the growth of governments and bureaucracies. To paraphrase, Parkinson opined that bureaucracies grow between two to five percent per year, regardless of the work being done or projected. He also theorized that work expands to fill the time allotted for its completion – highlighting the need to regularly review staffing levels and to set effective deadlines. These theories were first introduced in *The Economist* in the 1950s and continue to remain accurate for making broad predictions.

One past mentor, a former city manager, used to say that all some managers do is create more busy work. He may or may not have known about Parkinson's theories, but he was acknowledging one of the elements.

For the sake of argument, assume that Parkinson's Law is precisely correct. Leaders attempt to hire more subordinates to build their fiefdoms, demonstrate their value, and obtain more work so they can, in turn, hire even more employees. The challenge here is that future workload or revenue projections are imprecise – even if used – and governments rarely reduce their workforce voluntarily.

A leading reason for the theory's accuracy is that government agencies are run through a hierarchical work structure, some variation of a pyramid. That structure exists for clarity of authority and continuity of government operations. However, if agencies move further away from this structure, then inefficiencies start to emerge, which may take great energy to correct once in place.

In order to properly construct that pyramid, first, an appropriate span of control is needed. The span of control means the number of subordinates for each supervisor or manager. In municipal governments, it's typically a best practice to have a range of five to seven subordinates per supervisor at a minimum – with some unique exceptions. Additionally, it is important to eliminate one-to-one reporting relationships when focusing on efficient organizational structures.

For the movement of information, transparency, and systemic control, it's also more effective to have no more than five supervisory layers from the top to the bottom of an organization. That may seem a bit arbitrary, but without a target number on the total layers, people can just keep adding supervisors.

Why does that matter? With an excessive number of layers, for an employee to raise a material issue, they have to go through six or more different managers or supervisors to get to the leadership team. That is the beginning of what critics would call a bloated bureaucracy, and rightfully so. With a more compact organization, correct information can flow back and forth more easily, and there is more accountability with each supervisor. This generally results in greater alignment of the organization with the goals of leadership emanating from a clearer flow of information.

That being said, there are also multiple ways to construct an organization. Is the goal to have a team that can go off and build that bridge from cradle to grave? What about more specific functional or support units, like one handling just the inspection, design, or construction phase of a project?

There is not a right-or-wrong answer. The most effective structure depends on the type of work and the skill set of the employees. But while setting up that structure, consider whether the goal is to support cross-functional teams or teams responsible for a specific function.

IMPACT OF PARKINSON'S LAW

"...Work expands so as to fill the time available for its completion."

"...The number of [government] officials and the quantity of the work to be done are not related to each other at all. The rise in the total of those employed [by a government]...would be much the same whether the volume of work were to increase, diminish or even disappear."

*By C. Northcote Parkinson - from his article first appearing in The Economist in November 1955

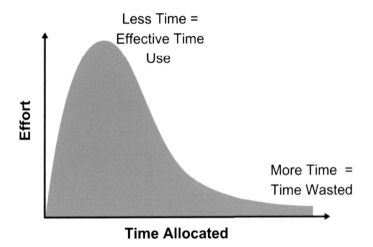

1. Efficient and effective organizational structures

2. Ambitious, but practical deadlines create pressure to avoid procrastination or filling time with trivial matters or overly in-depth analysis

3. Put projects, or key elements, into the context of larger goals or objectives with associated timelines developed with the smallest reasonable metric (i.e. days rather than weeks)

Focus on Efficiency

Establishing or altering the structure of an organization might be best achieved through an overriding focus on efficiency. That might sound simple, but as seen through the various hierarchical structures, a leader might have multiple options with answers that are neither right nor wrong.

Part of the efficiency focus is establishing fair, consistent, and market-compatible hourly rates or salaries. At first glance, that might seem like more of a private sector issue, but it also carries a surprising level of importance for municipalities.

Hourly rates are important for multiple reasons. These impact the cost of services provided to other departments utilizing different funding sources. Also, agencies may provide services to other entities outside of the organization or require time tracking for federally funded projects. Finally, many agencies provide development review and permitting services to their constituents, which may be charged through a time and materials-based fee structure – relying on appropriate and tolerable hourly rates.

Billing rate descriptions, and contributing costs, should be thorough and transparent. With federal or state funding, some of that money may be used to pay for the administrative costs of your agency, but the background data and backup calculations for hourly rates are important to support validating reimbursement requests.

ORGANIZATIONAL RESTRUCTURING

Before:

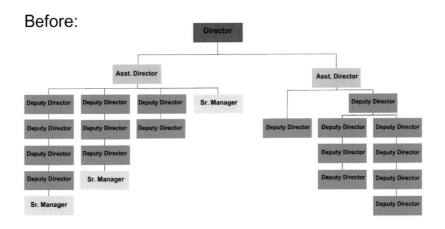

Span of Control: 5 to 7 subordinates per supervisor
Total Layers (top to bottom): Target 5 max
Eliminate 1 to 1 reporting relationships
Standardize Position Classifications
Align staff with groups that best fit career path / growth potential

After:

These factors are why it's important to consider organizational efficiencies and their effect on billing rates. Ultimately, somebody's going to see that hourly rate that the plumber or the inspector is charging with all of the overhead of your agency built into that rate. Striving for a pyramid-shaped structure will ultimately utilize fewer managers to deliver similar or greater workloads, resulting in a lower and more efficient hourly rate.

Impacts of Unions

Union representatives are like anyone else in that it's better to have their support (or neutrality) than their opposition. As with any negotiating partner, discerning their motivations can be pivotal in obtaining support. Unions are primarily funded through member dues. The more filled positions, the more dues they could ultimately collect.

It's important to remember that these collected funds are the fuel that propels their service to their members, including bargaining on employee contracts. For example, well-funded unions can, among other things, invest in political campaigns to elect officials sympathetic to their causes.

This sounds straightforward, but as with most issues in municipal government, it is a multi-layered world of often-competing interests. Union officials don't prioritize hourly rates used for billing, funding projections, or operational service levels. They prioritize position numbers, protecting employees, and negotiating employee benefits. This is not a criticism; it is simply a presentation of ideals to enhance empathy when working with them. The key is to provide them with information in advance and include union representatives in significant organizational discussions or events. Staying in regular contact might make union representatives more likely to listen to your ideas because you will have already developed some measure of productive relationships.

One specific issue with unions involves people hired for time-certain special projects or initiatives. What about hiring consultants or outsourcing work just for that project rather than hiring new employees? The goal should be balancing the need for union support with the benefits of external, ad hoc hires. Utilizing external consultants and resources can become a crucial tool to combat an expanding bureaucracy and avoid the otherwise inevitable results of Parkinson's Law. External resources are your hedge against fluctuating revenues and workloads. It is a partnership built through a symbiotic relationship. Some examples are highly specialized services like certain engineering or inspection services and almost all construction services.

Another factor is that government employees may not always have state-of-the-art training or technology expertise. As the fleet vehicles change over, employees might be used to turning screws and wrenches. When the cars eventually become computerized, and now they're behind the curve, then what are your options for those employees?

Alternatively, the private sector is required to keep up with the newest technology to stay relevant in business. This results from basic market forces at work – which governments tend to react to with delayed timelines.

This all goes back to the axiom that "the role of government is to do for the community what the people can't do for themselves." Sometimes government employees better understand the issue or the design genesis or standards rationale, but sometimes the delivery of work is best provided through other sources. Those decisions need to be made by leaders striving for an efficient and effective organization while not being blind to available external resources.

This brings us back to working with unions. Sometimes, despite consistently good communication, you might find yourself faced with extreme opposition from union representatives and just have to make the best of it. At Orange County, our massive organizational restructuring affected almost 200 positions via reclassifications to create standardization and address workload variations between business units.

The restructuring initiative also resulted in the elimination of 60 positions over a period of time, beginning with vacant positions. That was the easiest way to make early gains as there's no constituent for a vacant position, except for the union, and it's not directly affecting anybody personally when getting rid of a vacancy. It can sound draconian, but it can work if you're doing it strategically, and you may be forced to start somewhere due to an unforeseen meteor. This type of action can also have another impact. For example, you may experience an employee group complaining that they can't get something done due to a scenario of five vacant positions. Well, eliminating three of them and focusing on filling the remaining two creates a fully staffed outcome. Further, was there a recent objective analysis done that justified all five positions in the first place, or was that just status-quo thinking? Were the positions requested to be filled simply because they were vacant?

A situation may also arise wherein unions become allied with a new political candidate elected with an agenda counter to the direction that the agency might have been going. If you have partnered with unions all along and consistently explained the rationale for initiatives - why efficiency is important and why it is good for the health of the agency and, ultimately, it's employees - opposition might just be the result of disruption from the meteor of a political shift in ideology. In some cases, the strategic timing of an initiative is just as important as the resulting benefits.

4

FINANCES AND FUNDING

Taxes vs. fees

The distinction between taxes and fees is important for the leaders to know when concurrently interacting with elected officials, budget staff, or a chief financial officer on a new initiative. This is equally important when talking with people in the community because many proclaim with great zeal that they are not supportive of new taxes or even the existing tax structures. In many parts of America, an elected official saying otherwise (i.e., supporting taxation) is grounds for defeat at the ballot box. Thus, it is important to understand that asking for a tax adjustment can, even if reasonable and justified, be met with subjective and objective challenges.

The general fund of a government agency can pay for most of its needs because those funds come from sales taxes, property taxes, and all different taxes that a city or county levies at the local level, not assigned to a specific category. So that's great. Those funds are appropriately categorized as "general," are usually the most flexible, and can cover the largest number of budgetary needs.

Governments are primarily run via their tax revenues. Usually, debt service obligations are first in line, then followed by paying for law enforcement using general funds. Next comes the fire department. Afterward, the local government allocates general funds for community interests, e.g., parks, recreation services, community centers, and senior services.

Also, cities or counties will receive some allocation of gas tax dollars to pay for roadways, bridges, and operations and maintenance of those facilities. Finally, sales tax elements and hotel tax elements can pay for economic development or public transit and categories of that nature with a specific designation.

But the hard thing for people to think about regarding taxes is that it's often a zero-sum game. The community groups will say they don't want any more taxes, but they also will be the first to request more public pools or demand that their parks be better serviced or appeal to their elected officials for a police officer "on every corner."

That's the nuance. Correctly established fees improve a department's financial health because fees are direct payments for requested services. Also, elected officials usually don't care as much about fees because one can argue that a fee is linked to an individual making a specific request or receiving a direct service. For example, water and sewer services are paid for via fees. Accordingly, the individual's payments are variable and based on usage. Development services like permitting and plan review and tasks related to buildings by private developers or homeowners are also specific services, which usually are paid for with fees.

Reducing reliance on the general fund can increase the credibility of an agency because those actions free up money for the other portions of the larger organization that may not have another funding source.

Establishing a fee structure

One of the ways to reduce an agency's reliance on general funds is with an updated and comprehensive fee structure. When setting up this structure, make sure that it completely covers all the costs of the services provided under each fee category. Also, consider establishing a reserve fund to deal with the ups and downs of the economy to avoid using those general fund tax dollars to subsidize these services that are in place to facilitate private development or individualized requests.

A multi-layered fee structure analysis is recommended and needs to be periodically renewed to consider variables like inflation, consumer price indexes, and fluctuating staffing.

ORGANIZATIONAL STRUCTURE EFFECT ON BILLING RATES

Targeted Positions (with annualized costs)

<u>Manager</u> Salary $150,000 Fully Burdened Cost* $205,000
<u>Specialist</u> Salary $75,000 Fully Burdened Cost* $105,000

*Accounts for added costs associated with PTO, insurance and retirement benefits.

Results from various span of control scenarios:

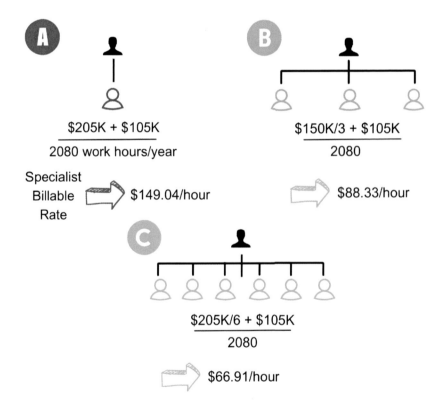

A

$205K + $105K
_____
2080 work hours/year

Specialist Billable Rate → $149.04/hour

B

$150K/3 + $105K
_____
2080

→ $88.33/hour

C

$205K/6 + $105K
_____
2080

→ $66.91/hour

Bonding, bond ratings, and debt service

A healthy general fund for a city or county is also a key ingredient in the recipe for a strong bond rating. In general, rating agencies assess the following factors for assigning a rating for general obligation bonds: Economy, Debt Structure, Financial Condition, Demographic Factors, and Management Practices of the governing body and its administration. Wall Street companies like Moody's and S&P Global set the bond rating for most agencies, with "AAA" being the best bond rating available.

Understandably, elected officials take pride in having a good bond rating for many reasons. First, it is a direct reflection of the financial health of the organization, and a strong bond rating allows a government to borrow money at a lower interest rate and save massive amounts in interest payments. It is important to understand this because, in an agency or department, organizational efficiency can contribute to creating an improved financial picture and help put more general fund dollars toward efforts to get a better bond rating.

For example, building a new city hall may include issuing bonds to finance it, as the total cost of the project cannot be afforded in a single fiscal year budget. Additionally, the degrading infrastructure conditions in the U.S. are constant reminders that most of the things that we utilize in the public realm today were built between the 1950s and the 1970s and were implemented with a roughly 50-year design life cycle. There are simply not enough annual funding amounts to address the level of investment necessary for public agencies to adequately update their infrastructure. This eventually leads to a discussion of financing and determining if the agency can afford the debt service of a long-term bond.

Debt service payments come right off the top of the ledger to pay for bond commitments before an agency can pay for operating costs or capital improvements. As bond ratings become increasingly important, so do the health trends of government budgets, which leads to finding efficiencies in annual budgets.

Zero-based budgeting

For capital projects, each year entails going through the project as part of a multi-year program, refining that budget, submitting it to the finance group of an agency, and ultimately presenting it to elected officials.

This is vastly different from the way budgeting is done for operational expenses, and zero-based budgeting starts with reviewing one fiscal year. In many governments, a common practice is a department taking the budget from a prior year, looking at the consumer price index or inflation trends, and adding a blanket percent increase to almost all line items from last year to develop the next fiscal year's budget. This approach may sound reasonable, but is it responsible? While this may be routine, there is a harder but more effective and accurate budgeting strategy.

Remember, the overall budget will only be approved at a certain level that the community or your agency can afford based on projected revenues and anticipated expenses. If almost every department submits a budget with blanket increases, maybe predicting that they will only get 90 percent of that, some funding will ultimately be allocated to cover arbitrary budget requests. This approach reduces the ability to fund other needs because some budgets will have been over-inflated.

For zero-based budgeting, consider splitting the budget into three categories: red, yellow, and green. "Red" represents things that are out of a department's control or cannot be impacted. That generally includes salaries, e.g., a built-in raise from a prior union negotiation. You are contractually required to pay those raises. Another example is the cost of your real estate - if the office has a lease contract built-in, you have to pay those costs. Don't expend too much energy focusing on those in the Red category.

Yellow signifies categories of things that have to be done but could be affected if you made some operational changes or introduced strategic efficiencies. One example is delaying the purchase of a new vehicle or making alternative transportation plans. These choices require holistic and multi-year thinking, and decisions may produce different results every year.

The Green categories include items that merit a full analysis are should initially be zeroed out at the beginning of the process. That's where the term "zero-based" budgeting comes from. You zeroed those out to force a full rebuild of those targeted budgetary line items.

Consider the example of paper purchases - if the paper budget last year was $5,000, one could zero that out and then justify the build-back of that budget by going out and getting an updated estimate for the cost of paper the next year. Additionally, usage trends should be reviewed, along with requesting that managers provide more information about actual operations linked to these utilizations. Maybe the department underwent an initiative to digitize most of the agency's documents. Would the department actually need greater funding for its paper budget the following year, even if the market cost of paper increased? A zero-based budgeting approach will produce a final operating budget with greater accuracy.

ZERO BASED BUDGETING

Fiscal Year Example for Operational Budget

	Salaries
	Retirement contributions
	Insurance
	Lease / rental payments

RED

*Beyond Department Control

	Vehicle purchases / fuel
	IT Equipment / licenses
	Overtime
	Contractural services
	Training

YELLOW

*Important, but could be impacted through process / procedure changes

	Paper
	Office supplies
	Food and beverages
	Travel and conferences

GREEN

*Most flexible, zero out and rebuild every year

Grants and federal funding

Countless sums are spent on the pursuit of grants each year, including costs for professional grant writers and advocacy efforts. The strategies of grant pursuits differ among governments, depending on regulations in their home state, their populations, and endless other factors. Unfortunately, most federal grants carry premium expenses and extended timelines that make them prohibitive for some mid to smaller-sized agencies.

For smaller governments, there is actually a way to ride the coattails of larger agencies in obtaining needed funds.

This strategy is known as the federal funding exchange program, which is primarily used in the transportation funding categories. Approximately 16 U.S. states currently have the authority to implement federal funding swaps or exchanges. The idea is to avoid those federal process premiums and reduced cost-benefit impacts.

The premise is that a local agency can, in some states, exchange federal funding allocations with a larger agency or different agency in their region and get local (non-federal) money in return. That local money is "clean," meaning that there are no additional audits or requirements other than any local regulations of the respective city or state.

That creates a significant advantage for smaller agencies that might receive federal funding like the stimulus dollars of 2009, Covid emergency funding, or allocations from the recent infrastructure acts.

For example, if a state agency was delivering a $50 million project that was receiving federal funds, they're already taking on the burden of the federal process premiums. Those become sunk costs, and so any additional federal money they receive doesn't increase their burden.

But swapping those dollars benefits the larger receiving agency because they get more money beyond original allocations or grant award amounts. They've already addressed the federal burden and, if they exchange local funds back to that smaller agency, now that smaller agency receives supplemental funding that is free from federal requirements. An exchange rate between agencies is typically negotiated and so contacting a professional who is experienced in navigating this process is recommended.

Centennial Way - Phoenix, AZ: Streetscape initiative utilizing federal funding and had an unmovable completion date.

5

PROGRAMMING AND PLANNING

For new leaders, multi-year projects like major roads and bridges can be a daunting undertaking. These consume many years of planning and stakeholder engagement to begin implementation and to complete these multi-phased efforts. If agencies are not aligned in those phases and focused on the ultimate delivery of that project, the process can become unwieldy and extremely inefficient.

Government agencies generally only approve a budget that covers a single fiscal year. This cycle is typically either a July 1 start, a January 1 start, or aligned with the federal fiscal year, which has traditionally been on an October 1 start. When coordinating with CFOs or budget directors, their primary focus may be that an elected body only approves a budget for a single year. There are some cases wherein agencies approve a two-year budget but include breakdowns for each year.

That targeted focus is understandable; however, capital

improvement projects almost always last well beyond a single year. That's why it's important to develop and maintain a multi-year capital improvement program.

Capital improvement programs

Key components are the project cost estimates, the project phases, and the placement within the overall multi-year program. The budget supporting the current year's project cost elements of the program is typically approved as part of the single fiscal year actions. A project phase details where the money's going to be spent independent of time for that project element. The program is how you plan for those project phases, in accordance with the annual budget process, over multiple years to organize funding for the delivery of that entire project.

If agency leaders are not programming out applicable costs for all of the projects over multiple years - and generally, capital improvement programs are five, seven, or ten years - then there will likely be funding challenges. You won't be able to line up annual funding allocations in a way where you can address valleys or peaks in your capital improvement program expenditures and ensure these are covered with available resources.

Hypothetically, suppose a project needs two million dollars in year one for the design phase. Next comes the need for three million dollars in year two for land acquisition. Finally, ten million dollars is required in year three to build the project.

What if the annual allocated revenues only total five million dollars? In year one, when spending two million, three million should be placed in reserve. In year two, when spending three million, two million should be placed in reserve. Under this strategy, five million lies in reserve by the time you get to year three, and then there is a total of ten million dollars available to construct the project. That's a simple example of how to deliver a ten-million-dollar construction project with only five million in annual revenues.

However, multiple construction projects hitting at the same time could easily wipe out the annual funding allocations and reserve amounts. That's why it's very important to have a comprehensive capital improvement program, and it is crucial to help accountants and budget directors understand the importance of having a multi-year program established. Thankfully, programs are typically available as a planning strategy under most municipal operations and can be approved separately as a program and not a standalone budget.

A recommended strategy is for the agency's elected body to approve a refined version of the program each year. It's important to provide reminders each year that the elected body has seen and approved prior versions and that

CAPITAL IMPROVEMENT PROGRAMS

Capital improvement programs should cover 5, 7 or 10 year periods. The example below demonstrates how to layout out a single project.

Project Phases	Fiscal Year 1	Fiscal Year 2	Fiscal Year 3
Construction Cost Estimate			$10,000,000
Pre-Design	$200,000		
Design	$1,400,000		
Design Admin/ Project Mgmt	$100,000	$100,000	$100,000
Survey - Design	$400,000		
Survey - Construction			$400,000
Environmental Permits	$200,000	$300,000	
Utilities		$400,000	
Right of Way		$2,000,000	
Construction Mgmt			$1,200,000
Environmental Mitigation			$500,000
Total	$2,300,000	$2,800,000	$12,200,000

Publishing annual updates to a fiscally constrained and resource balanced capital improvement program can increase the rate at which project phases are successfully delivered within budget time frames.

they understand the need to approve it again to include annual updates and create alignment on projected future expenditures.

Fiscally constrained and resource balanced

Just putting a capital improvement program out there is great, but two things need to be strongly considered to maximize its effectiveness and success. One is the fiscal constraint based on the analysis of projected revenues against ongoing expenses. It can be common for agencies to put their plans on a sheet of paper and project their expenses, but the fiscal constraint strategy includes looking at revenues coming in and then constraining your program every year by offsetting your revenue projections against ongoing expenditures (like routine operations and maintenance) to avoid going over budget. Aside from the projection of project expenses, this effort also requires a long-term projection of annual revenues and forecasting of market trends. This analysis also helps maximize the use of allocated funds in any given year of the program.

Next is resource balancing. The available people and associated resources to deliver projects should be considered to determine how many projects can be expected for delivery per year. With the utilization of all the staff or private sector resources, if only five projects a year can be delivered, then

Avenida La Pata - Orange County, CA: Massive transportation project that required a strategic multi-year funding plan.

beware of a program that proposes seven projects a year because that's likely overpromising results and creates risk associated with the agency's performance.

Resource-balancing the program includes a more focused approach to aligning the activities of internal human resources and leveraging external vendor partners. This can also help with credibility because the goal is to deliver on the agency's stated program commitments.

Every project is judged by basically three things:

Did the project deliver the usable or tangible elements it was supposed to include? For example, did it construct five miles of road with a six-lane bridge? Was it completed within the published schedule? Did its costs remain within the assigned budget? Meeting all three of those criteria begets a winning project that improves the credibility of your organization in an objective manner. Failure in any one of those components risks undermining that credibility and may trigger inquiries from elected officials or the public.

Leaders can increase the likelihood of success by utilizing owner's advisors - experts in the specific type of project or in the implementation of capital programming strategies. These external representatives can also advise on projects that a department has never handled before. If the city hall is 70 years old and no current leaders have ever handled the construction of a city hall, this creates a prime situation for accessing the wisdom of an experienced owner's advisor. Personally, serving as an owner's advisor has provided an

Edinger Bridge - Huntington Beach, CA: Emergency replacement requiring ferries to maintain access during construction.

avenue to make a significant difference for local agencies by lending deep knowledge from decades of experience.

Transparency of a project's completion

Some residents may exclaim - Why is our city government spending all of the money in other parts of town? What about our neighborhood? Shouldn't we matter since we pay taxes too? Is this just about politics?

Although these questions may be common, there is a chance to avoid them if people fully understand all categories of work being done in "their part of town." Part of being a leader in a government agency is letting the community know about the great work being done – which could be maintenance activities - to improve the areas where they live, work, and play. It might not be spelled out in the job description, but informing the public should stand tall on the list of goals for an effective government leader.

For many agencies, the projects or initiatives highly visible to the public might include buildings, roads, bridges, flood control facilities, or drainage basins. However, they could also include lesser seen infrastructure elements, like a wastewater treatment plant.

State Capitol Building - Phoenix, AZ: The pathway to the Capitol has historic elements and visibility restrictions.

Groundbreaking and ribbon-cutting events

These events are another part of leadership that some people might dismiss as all about politics or grandstanding. However, events of this type are great for the community as a whole and offer a public forum to highlight the objective efforts of your agency.

At the end of the day, elected officials love these occasions to get out in front of their constituents with a positive message. In planning for these events, consider giving your elected officials a chance, a public relations opportunity, to kick off or celebrate the completion of a project or major initiative. This creates a winning scenario, wherein the participants feel good about the day, and credibility continues to build for your agency, which will likely be needed in the future when another project doesn't go as well.

What some people miss is that this effort also benefits the community, and they can help celebrate the event. Groundbreakings bring a sense of hope that, in a small way, signifies this day as a step toward a shade brighter future or improved neighborhood. For ribbon-cuttings, it's the celebration of the good that government can do and a commemoration that quality of life has just improved by some measure. That is especially true if the project has been disruptive by bringing construction noise or dust into their lives for a season of time. The community can now celebrate that the inconvenience is over and that the gain was worth all the temporary pain.

While it might appear or even feel political, highlighting successful project deliveries increase public trust in government, boost morale, and can give the public greater insight into how their tax dollars have been spent.

Orange County, CA: This legacy ribbon cutting event accommodated more than 4,000 guests and numerous local venders.

6

PROCUREMENT AND PARTNERING

Procurement processes are the way in which a government agency acquires external services and commodities. This is a critical government process, inviting the private sector to provide goods to, or services on behalf of, the public agency. These often include but are not limited to services from planners, architects, engineers, and construction contractors.

A government agency procures external resources through the release of documents, e.g., requests for interest, requests for qualifications, requests for proposals, requests for bids, or equipment requisitions directed to the private sector.

Sometimes contracts are awarded based solely on price, and others are selected based on qualifications or a combination of both. No matter the criteria, each bears a different type of risk because whenever the private sector competes, the result is the creation of winners and losers. No one likes to lose, and, within the losing companies, whoever prepared the proposal might try to direct blame toward the government to justify the failure. Government agencies present an easy target, including a convenient claim that politics was the reason that a proposal failed to be selected.

Sadly, even well-orchestrated procurement processes with fair results can be discredited by unsuccessful parties.

If that sounds unfair to the public agency, that's because it is. If a leader is not focused on procurement strategies, and their quality and consistency, substantial risk can be created. A department can get blindsided by something that was thought to be standard, but a portion of the process hadn't been updated. Maybe it didn't comply with a recent state law change or agency policy, or maybe the administering staff required more training than the leaders thought.

Additional red flags include the duration of the process. That's important because if things take too long, the result can be a loss of credibility, and it's easy to criticize governments for being slow. Also, proposing firms may be contributing to political campaigns for elected officials, and they may provide direct unfiltered feedback with limited context. That could ultimately result in top-down pressure because the process didn't meet the practical test of how fast it should be.

The second red flag involves levels of oversight. Generally, government bureaucrats love more layers of authority for perceived checks and balances. The more authority delegated to a leader and their agency, in general,

Arizona State University Comms Building - Phoenix, AZ: Utilized the Construction Manager At-Risk delivery method.

the faster operational processes can go. The more oversight there is, the slower the process goes. Also, governments will inevitably conduct audits. What happens every time there's an audit? Are there more rules put into place or fewer rules?

An audit almost always introduces more rules and checkpoints. Auditing a process every three years, while well-intentioned, is likely to add more rules or process steps. Sometimes those additional checkpoints are good, but they typically reduce the speed of the process.

Also, all these things can diminish the authority of a leader, as slow processes can be perceived as clumsy or unorganized. That's why it's so important to focus on efficiency because audits or the impact of people's complaints will only add more inefficiencies to your process. The goal should be a balance of standardized procedures, with basic hierarchical oversight, for implementing the most efficient process.

Partnering with the private sector

The private sector has a window into the procurement process once a solicitation is published. It is important to partner with the private sector because it is productive to have concerned constituents, especially vocal ones, interact with government leaders in private before speaking publicly in a negative way. Another reason is obtaining input on how efficient and effective the process is and whether people feel the process is clear and fair.

Animal Care Facility - Tustin, CA: Utilized the Design-Build delivery method for speed and to finish within the budget.

Also, positive relationships with private sector companies can become crucial when meteors appear. Suppose there's an emergency like a flood or a collapsed bridge. Good partners in the private sector can come to aid in helping solve some of those major issues or problems, like the need for additional resources. Moreover, these partners can provide sophistication and stability if their businesses have been properly supported via a reasonable winning percentage for government procurements within the competitive local markets.

Selection Panels

It's important to have diversity in selection panels as part of a public procurement process, including a variety of internal departments with general knowledge of the services. It is also wise to include, on those panels, industry experts in providing the service being evaluated, either from the private sector or from another proximate public agency.

Extensive experience on selection panels is also important because the members will benefit from people who have been through the process before. It is also important to have an odd number of people on the panel to avoid voting ties.

On-call contracts for professional services

The on-call contracts for various professional service categories are established through a request for qualifications. This is a request for the best engineers for bridges, the best architects for buildings, the best designers for flood control facilities, etc., from which the agency creates a slate of on-call qualified firms and may award multiple capped capacity contracts for future – yet unknown - projects. When the need arises, the agency can go right to those firms to issue a task order to deliver design phases or analyses in support of a project. There is no need to re-procure because the department has already procured those services via a prior selection process. On-call contracts of this nature are typically used for smaller projects or for pieces of the design phase for larger projects since they were selected under design categories with limited specific project details.

Innovations to Improve Project Delivery

The construction phase is the biggest cost component of any project in almost every case. Typically, agencies are experienced in acquiring those services through a price-based selection. You're going to request bids, and the lowest bid wins. It has been happening that way for hundreds of years. That sounds simple, but this simplicity does not account for various factors which can create huge risks.

Anyone reading this book likely hopes to find insight and strategies born from decades of experience. Would a wise person purchase a book from another author, who has minimal applicable experience, just because the retail price of that book was a few dollars cheaper?

With that example in mind, let's examine the deception of selection by purely the lowest price. Generally, the only required qualifications are a state-issued license for the submitting general contractor. Someone who paid for a license but may have limited applicable experience can create many challenges for complicated projects. Unfortunately, these are not overtly considered by many agencies when selecting services for the largest financial piece of the project.

Then, those agencies are surprised when a project doesn't go well. This is especially true if schedule adherence is not prioritized or complications arise beyond the scope of the contractor's ability to resolve them.

A bid for construction services may provide the initial lowest price, but that number is ultimately unlikely to be the final price. Projects procured with low-bid methods often result in a demand for more money because of newly discovered facts or lack of clarity. This is generally followed by a denial of more money by the public agency, a lawsuit against the agency, and finally, a mediated settlement between the parties or the rendering of a legal judgment.

Santa Ana River Sand Management Project - Newport Beach, CA: Utilized the Construction Manager At-Risk delivery method.

Bid, build, claim, litigate, and then settle. That's the pathway on which many big complex construction projects usually end up.

APDMs: There is another way

Alternate Project Delivery Methods, or APDMs, offers alternatives to the traditional low-bid procurement process.

These tend to be more progressive delivery methods, and some may require state-enabling legislation. Federal agencies sometimes have the authorization to utilize these methods, whereas every city or county across the country may only have the ability or procedures in place to select services based on the lowest price.

Contracts for design services are typically awarded on a qualifications-based selection. This selection type is good and appropriate for selecting a designer like a structural engineer to build a bridge. If the bridge collapses, no agency wants to answer questions on why they selected the cheapest structural engineer. That is why qualifications are the primary factor in selecting design services, and APDMs bring this approach into the process for selecting construction phase services.

Design-build

Design-Build is usually applied to the most complex projects or when speed of project delivery is prioritized.

This method involves the government agency selecting a prime contractor, including a team with its designer, and all the services necessary to deliver that project under one contract. The agency selects that team through a combination of qualifications, similar project references, and a proposed project approach. Design-Build may also include a minor price component – if implemented correctly.

A higher or exclusive focus on qualifications can receive pushback from low-bid contractors or traditionalists. However, the design-build process is built off of partnerships and seeks to minimize conflicts while identifying risks early on. After the design phase, the next step for the agency is to negotiate with the prime contractor to develop a guaranteed maximum price that will form the final elements of the contract. Because the agency, the designer, and the contractor are working together toward a common goal, conformance to a guaranteed maximum price, including the transfer of risk, can be achieved - somewhat enhanced by the strategic use of allowances and contingencies. All of these efforts add greater schedule and cost predictability than the traditional low-bid selection method.

Construction manager at risk

Another of the alternative project delivery methods is termed Construction Manager At-Risk or CMAR. The reason it's called a construction manager "at risk" is that the prime contractor is being inserted into the design phase as a construction manager to create a guaranteed maximum price. Once that price is negotiated for the construction phase services, the prime contractor then accepts the risk associated with project delivery because they participated in the process to establish the total price. This method is also sometimes called Construction Manager / General Contractor or CM/GC since the prime contractor acts as a construction manager during the design phase and then converts to a general contractor during the construction phase.

This method has similar benefits to Design-Build but requires two separate procurements. First, there is a process to select the engineer/architect to provide design services under the direction of the agency. Then, a second procurement process results in the addition of a Construction Manager At-Risk to the project. These two private sector entities work together, and with the public agency, in the pre-construction phase to develop a guaranteed maximum price. Once negotiated, the designer and the contractor report directly to the agency throughout the delivery of the project.

ALTERNATE PROJECT DELIVERY METHODS

Design-Build

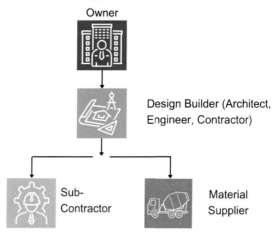

Owner

Design Builder (Architect, Engineer, Contractor)

Sub-Contractor

Material Supplier

Construction Manager At-Risk

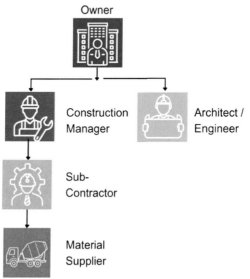

Owner

Construction Manager

Architect / Engineer

Sub-Contractor

Material Supplier

The Construction Manager At-Risk delivery method takes a little bit longer because there are two separate procurements. However, public agencies may feel it gives them more control because the designers, architects, and engineers report directly to the owner. Those services don't all report to the prime contractor as in the Design-Build process.

Job order contracting

A third method is termed Job Order Contracting or JOC. Similar to the process described earlier in a prior chapter for on-call professional service contracts, JOCs can also be established through a request for qualifications, which may include a price component depending upon applicable state laws. In some states, bids for line item construction categories are requested and scored on the lowest, weighted prices. JOCs are effectively on-call construction services and are typically awarded as capped capacity contracts for future – yet unknown – construction or maintenance projects. As needed, the agency can utilize JOCs to deliver construction-type services for a project or initiative. JOCs are typically used for smaller projects or maintenance activities since they were selected under construction categories with limited specific project details. Having contracts like this in place can be a game changer for agencies and boost credibility due to significant decreases in response time to address urgent issues requiring construction services.

7

EFFICIENCIES AND ENERGY

This chapter is intended to deliver insight into the micro, day-to-day issues and decisions that can prepare you for those unknown meteors headed toward your agency. The focus is on operational efficiencies, which can create ongoing impacts and benefits.

Technology upgrades are at the top of the list, largely because they are one of the many tasks with which public agencies struggle and require ongoing efforts to stay up to date. The process to implement a technology solution can take years, including months needed for soliciting a technology, reviewing proposals, coordinating selection panels, doing product demos, testing the system, and then facilitating "go-live" procedures.

This is not exactly government at its best. While trying to set up your standards and select a technology, that technology category continues to improve or evolve. In many cases, the day that a government organization turns on the switch to their new solution, that technology has already aged to some extent.

Enterprise License Agreements

One strategy to understand when you're looking at a technology solution is the contractual mechanism of Enterprise License Agreements or ELAs. While one department might need this technology, other departments may also utilize the solution if the product was contracted with an ELA.

Paying a premium for an enterprise license agreement means that anybody in your enterprise or agency has access to it through its licensing approach. Thus, paying that premium sometimes can have an efficiency halo effect because other departments are getting the technology at a significantly reduced cost or for free in some cases.

That's one avenue. The other is that with an enterprise license agreement, the department dealing with the technical challenge may be able to get funding from other sources or departments if its own funds are limited. Taking an enterprise-wide approach to technology, and spreading the costs, can be advantageous but can also offer standardization to workflows or business processes.

Software as a Service

The next industry term to know on the technology side is Software as a Service or SaaS. Instead of making a capital investment and buying permanent one-time licenses, the department pays on a monthly or yearly subscription basis to access the software virtually. In addition to the benefit of dialing up or down your software subscription user numbers as needed, the technology solution receives instantaneous product updates due to its virtual connectivity for accessing base program elements.

OTS vs. Customization

OTS represents an "off the shelf" strategy, meaning the technology solution is purchased in whole and without modification. Just plug it in and use it. Alternatively, customized approaches involve a software developer building a one-of-a-kind solution with input from the agency. The software is customized to meet specific needs and solve unique agency challenges. That sounds great, but it generally costs a lot more money for that customization which can quickly get out of date. And, when the time comes for an update, that update also may be customized and rely on resources no longer accessible to the agency.

What if the software developer who did the customized programming is no longer with the company? What if the technology or business process has changed beyond the capabilities of the customized version? The more strategic alternative for governments is to buy off-the-shelf products and adjust internal business practices to align with the base software elements. Additionally, agencies can more objectively rate those solutions, easily obtain software updates, and better predict future annualized costs.

Asset management

Effective and efficient asset management requires consistent attention and careful planning. This includes trying to ascertain the condition of assets and what needs to be done to maintain those at a service level that's acceptable to users. For the leader, it's important to understand that not maintaining current assets will give rise to taxpayer complaints. With certain assets that have structural components, like roads or bridges, failing to properly maintain them can launch you into replacement mode, which usually involves major capital expenditures. In this section, the world of asset management for infrastructure has been divided into two categories: horizontal and vertical assets.

Horizontal asset management normally includes the fully public realm, meaning roads, bridges, flood control facilities, sidewalks, and parks. Those are accessible to the public and can degrade pretty quickly based on their use and levels of routine maintenance. In some cases, there are requirements to have an asset management program in place to successfully pursue federal dollars, depending upon the funding source. Finally, an important part of an asset management plan includes having a maintenance schedule that pushes out the replacement of that asset as far as possible while also funding a reserve for full reconstruction.

The vertical side of asset management normally includes high-value facilities like buildings. Normally, the buildings of an agency either serve as the work site for employees or as parking structures for public and private vehicles. By their nature, vertical assets are different because public feedback may be minimal due to limited access leading to long-term neglect. However, the safety of buildings can be called into question if those assets are not being managed properly. At that point, the resolution of the situation may be well beyond a quick fix. Vertical assets can also include ventilation systems, energy systems, air filtration systems, and other supporting equipment in buildings,

One simple example is the lighting systems within a building. Changing out old lighting systems to updated LED technology, which is very efficient, costs much more upfront than typical traditional replacement bulbs. One option is to keep using legacy lighting systems, which have a lower initial purchase price. However, they utilize more energy and are required to be replaced more often. A properly established asset management plan can provide trend data to aid with making these types of expenditure decisions.

Fleet Services

Most government agencies have a fleet. They include stock such as garbage trucks, bulldozers, and passenger vehicles the government agency uses just to get around, as well as fire and police equipment.

Certain challenges are associated with heavy equipment, fire, and police vehicles. By the time the base model is up-fit to become a police-ready vehicle, the cost will have likely doubled due to specialized equipment and the preferences of the users. Then add the labor to install all of the internal gear, equipment, and technology to make it a fully functioning public safety vehicle.

Another issue that many overlook is the routine maintenance of vehicles. Are employees available and trained to maintain those vehicles, or should a third party be contracted to service those vehicles? One way to mitigate some of these challenges is fleet vehicle standardization.

Consider your personal vehicle. The longer it is used, the more wear and tear it incurs. Along with that degradation comes less efficient gas mileage and lower safety ratings compared to new models with the latest technology. Even the sound systems will be worse as the vehicle becomes increasingly out of alignment with current standards.

As a leader, it is important to establish, update, and maintain a replacement schedule to move from a break-fix situation to a proactive fleet management strategy.

FLEET STANDARDIZATION

Strategic replacement of fleet vehicles reduces overall costs including downtime, maintenance and repairs, fuel usage, and safety risks.

Five vehicle fleet example

Annual 20% vehicle replacement leads to a modernized fleet in 5 years

Year 1	Year 2	Year 3	Year 4	Year 5

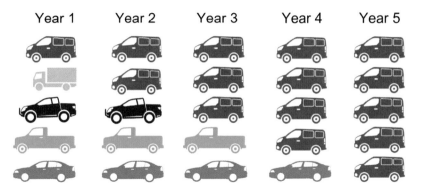

Benefits of modernizing and standardizing a fleet

✓ Mechanics are able to specialize on fewer vehicle types

✓ Less variation in parts leads to a higher volume per part which generates bulk discounts

✓ Reduced labor costs through focused training and minimized experience gaps

✓ Increased fuel efficiencies and utilization of warranty periods

✓ Progress toward compliance with zero emission vehicle mandates

The same principle applies to vehicle component parts. As the fleet becomes standardized, the associated parts can also be standardized. This results in dropping overhead costs because you're ordering a higher volume of the same parts for fewer types of vehicles.

All fleets are aging each day, and replacement costs will likely come from the general fund if the costs cannot be accommodated through operational department budgets. Without significant planning, agencies are unlikely to launch a successful standardization/replacement plan due to the lack of available funding. For a vehicle that's ten years old, it will be far less fuel efficient than a new vehicle in that same classification, parts will be outside of most warranty limits, and it will be unlikely to have the latest safety features. Recall the importance of reducing financial pressures on the general fund discussed in prior chapters – fleet modernization is an operational issue that could benefit from strategies that may take a longer return on investment.

Vehicle telematics

This technology is available and, generally, now a standard for many new vehicles, allowing an agency to get remote information from the vehicle in a digital format. The data is downloadable and also provides the ability to geographically locate fleet vehicles.

It might sound like a simple and easy decision to

embrace this technology; however, the use of telematics can quickly become a union issue and may generate employee pushback. Unions and individual employees may complain about the government trampling on their privacy rights. Also, operating and maintaining the systems comes at an additional cost.

If this technology is introduced, more questions may arise. Who has access to the data on the individuals using the vehicles? With whom may the agency share that information? If data reveals a possible violation of employee conduct or even a possible crime, who is authorized to investigate? Regarding employee conduct, who is the person with the authority to hear, read, and weigh the evidence to determine whether a violation has occurred? If so, what rights does the employee have to appeal this finding? The questions and the associated issues can turn a productive technology into new headaches for a leader. Still, vehicle telematics allows for the enhanced maintenance of the fleet due to real-time diagnostics (like braking and fuel efficiency) and provides the agency with the geographic location of its more costly assets.

Parking

As with fleet vehicle management, public and employee parking is another function that doesn't have a direct educational track or organized academic training. Experts develop knowledge about this industry segment by working through issues and first-hand experiences. Management of parking structures and setting applicable rates is both art and science. This is not to be overlooked because these structures represent a huge asset for a leader to oversee. In many cases, parking systems get less review and oversight than other department sections and may be taken for granted.

Much like asset management for buildings, this asset involves a combination of access to public and private spaces. Although parking structures or parking lots are public assets, customers and employees may park in the same facility. This interaction usually requires a stratified parking rate structure and can raise security concerns for an agency's employees.

Also, parking structures are a major outdoor asset routinely impacted by varied weather conditions. If that weren't enough, wear and tear is received from vehicles which also introduces structural strains unique to the facility management space.

Often, progressive agencies will move the accounting for these assets out of the general fund ledger. A parking system fund will be established with reliance on the parking system to fund those structures and associated future operations separately as an enterprise. This is an effective strategy so long as the agency is diligent about preventative maintenance and upkeep of those parking facilities. The reason is that

CATEGORIZATION OF PARKING RATES

1. Parking Violations

Highest per hour conversion rate priced at a level to encourage compliance

2. On-Street Parking Meters

Second highest per hour conversion rate to account for location convenience and to trigger turnover of spaces

3. Structures (Hourly)

Baseline for setting all rates and should be set to cover capital construction of the facility plus operations and maintenance costs

4. Structures (Monthly Permits)

Least expensive rate with least convenient location in lots or structures parking structures can cost roughly fifty thousand dollars per space to construct, depending on the geography and how they're built.

The big issue for a new leader is to understand that many believe all parking should be provided for free. Even if no charge is levied, there is no such thing as "free" parking due to construction, operations, maintenance, security, and equipment costs. Assuming that the parking structures will require customer payment for use, discerning and implementing appropriate rates and fees becomes another major challenge. The rates must be comparable to similarly situated municipalities (or private facilities). A city like Chicago may charge $50 per hour for parking; however, absent some extraordinary circumstances, most cities' rates will not approach that amount. Other issues that arise include enforcement of parking violations, monthly permit rates, group discounts, and coordination with proximate on-street parking meter rates.

Legitimate or not, parking can also become a personnel issue. Most employee groups typically say two things: *"Don't mess with our office space, and don't mess with our parking."*

Utility and Energy Management

For larger agencies within denser developed areas and with several facilities in close proximity, a strategy to consider is the generation or control of its energy through solar systems, an on-site co-generation plant, or an off-site central utility facility.

Managing one's own energy versus buying it from a local provider does produce a cost-benefit. There are, however, significant challenges. The need for constant monitoring may be obvious, beginning with the consequences of a failing power system during business hours. This issue should be carefully considered, especially if the agency is managing vertical assets through a break / fix methodology versus a proactive maintenance/replacement plan. Another challenge is strategically analyzing to insource or outsource plant operators and, of course, backup power plans. If something goes wrong, more than just the ability to service customers is lost as the workers in buildings connected to the power source lose productivity. Naturally, this situation creates bad headlines and causes countless other issues, not the least being reduced credibility of your organization.

The threshold question is whether to develop an off-grid power source with high upfront costs and lower ongoing energy costs or to connect to the local utility provider and pay higher energy costs on a monthly basis. The advice here is to tread carefully into this arena that entails at least as many challenges as there are benefits.

Reports and presentations to elected officials

Generally, cities have elected city councils, and counties have an elected board of supervisors. As city councils may increase based upon population changes, typically, there are more city council members than board of supervisor members. County boards of supervisors generally have five elected officials, whereas city councils could have all the way up to nine members.

Why is this important? Staff reports provide the chance to mold the image of a department or agency as the product will be presented in public forums and become a public record. Because so much of a department's work generally occurs beyond the public view, construction projects, and customer services become a boots-on-the-ground presence that the public can informally see and experience. When it comes to staff reports in public meetings, that's a formal setting. The attendees are more highly tuned into what's happening or what's being discussed. This is an important opportunity to further define the department's reputation and image.

This might come as a surprise, but public reporting to elected bodies can also be enhanced by operational efficiencies. Some of the benefits include 1) composing standardized reports; 2) using language and terms, along with the report's layout, that has become routine and comfortable for the elected officials; 3) utilization of a familiar style and substance to induce less skepticism and scrutiny; 4) media members who routinely cover meetings will quickly become familiar with the report format, allowing them to focus on the ultimate conclusions, and be more willing to use your reports as source material; and 5) consistent formats will allow you to quickly reference and answer questions about past reports if an elected official asks about something contained in a previous one.

A former California senator once advised me that someone presenting a report in a public forum should *"be brief, be brilliant, and be gone."* Wise advice intended to remind agency leaders to get to the point clearly and quickly.

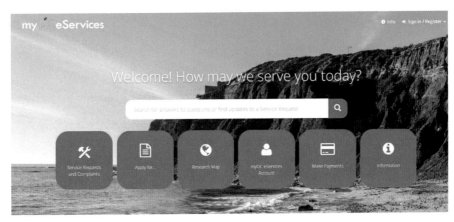

Orange County, CA: This online portal and software introduced the agency's first 24/7 virtual customer service system.

8

CUSTOMERS AND COMMUNITIES

When agencies publish a fee for a service, those paying for the service should be considered as customers, even in a government, non-profit scenario. Processing private development permit requests is a common situation where customer service is necessary. Handling financial transactions as part of this service also involves data security, quality, and physical safety considerations.

Anyone can say they are committed to customer service, but focusing on efficient processes and user-friendly interfaces should result in fewer complaints and greater agency credibility. A reputation for outstanding customer service can also help with getting approval for expenditures on technology upgrades or additional staffing if the goal is to enhance services to local constituents.

If advocating a governing body for a new or expanded program, effective messaging might be: "This is a customer service initiative, and implementing this system is how we can better help our constituents." This could buoy support from an elected body because it's hard to argue against improving customer service. This small change in the language of a report or presentation might just win the day.

Another strategy in developing a pro-customer-service culture is to change portions of a department traditionally called "divisions" to be called "service areas." The word division obviously implies a divide, while service areas direct one's focus toward a customer service mindset. This has worked well in the past because the agency's change in priorities and new initiatives aligns with this updated terminology. Additionally, service areas are a reminder to also serve colleagues or co-workers within the department and people in other agencies – not just the public.

Impacts of Subsidies

A more complicated but important decision revolves around the practice of subsidizing. Should an agency subsidize services or not? What does that mean? A subsidy is when a government agency uses another source of funds, usually general fund dollars, to reduce the published fee to the customer for something like processing a building permit. Suppose a resident goes to a public agency to get a building permit for a fee of $1,000 to construct a garage for their house. That permit processing fee could be reduced to $500 if that local agency wants to use general fund dollars to defray part of the operational expenses. However, most strategic agencies will want to reduce those subsidies because general fund dollars are in high demand, as discussed in previous chapters.

When utilizing a service, like development-related services, the requested action or access to that government agency is for an individual's specific request or a private purpose. Should revenues generated from the taxes of the entire population of a community be used to offset these individualized requests for services?

Many times, fees get subsidized through political oversight or due to a test of reasonableness. If a constituent thinks that the cost is just too high to get your water heater permit issued, the answer to that may be subsidizing. To this point, a city in California subsidizes up to 50 percent of its permit fees because they argue an economic development approach. More permitting activity is theoretically going to drive more development with the potential to generate more future tax dollars back to the public agency. Thus, the city's general fund picks up half of the total cost to provide those services.

At the end of the day, reducing the subsidies for these services supporting private investments can directly free up some general fund dollars. While maybe a little complicated for new leaders, it's important to understand what the percentage is that you're subsidizing when providing development services and the impact that this will have on your annual budgetary requests.

Fee structures should also be considered when evaluating published rates with the goal to maximize revenues to cover the total cost of providing government services. The fee for providing these services can either be a flat fee or a time and material fee. Most audits would encourage the use of time and material fees so the customer can understand that the ultimate cost is directly linked to the time it takes to process development submittals.

However, the other argument is that flat fees tend to be better for customers because it creates predictability. A hybrid approach might work best to provide baseline predictability but also allow for the fact that not all garages (in this example) are created equal. Some may have air-conditioning, heated floors, and an extensive sound system for entertainment – thus driving up the time necessary to review construction plans.

What about the development philosophy that is politically supported in a city or county? There is no right or wrong answer – only different approaches. In pro-development communities, the expectation will be to have as few regulations as possible other than what's absolutely necessary for legal compliance. Speed in providing development services will also be prioritized along with built-up staffing capacities to process high submittal volumes. The communities may not care as much about the fees from a cost standpoint, or they may want to subsidize them if they're trying to drive economic development.

IMPACTS OF SUBSIDIES ON FEES FOR SERVICES

50% fee subsidy example:

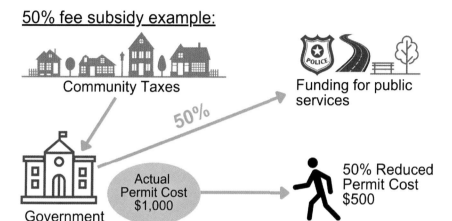

0% fee subsidy example:

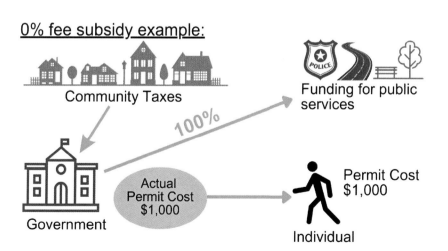

In a regulatory-focused community, a lot of the approaches are the opposite. In some cases, the fees are not an issue there either, but extra caution is expected around the permitting process, including adherence to more extensive local regulations or policies. Usually, a slower process also involves more environmental constraints or oversight reviews from other agencies or public committees. Customer service, while important on an individual level, is secondary in this case to a regulatory focus on the development processes for issuing building permits.

The key point is that it is important for a new leader to know which environment prevails in a given community because different factors will be of varied importance. Is that difference pretty quickly apparent when you come to a new area? It should be. Phoenix, Las Vegas, and Atlanta are regularly in the top group of cities in the country, issuing the greatest number of building permits every year. So those communities are supportive of development and growth. Generally, higher regulatory environments like those found in New York, California, and Washington prevail within communities closer to the coasts.

Whether on the coasts or in the middle of the country, understanding the focus of culture around private development can be crucial to a public sector leader's success.

Civic Space Park - Phoenix, AZ: Project transformed the downtown area with necessary green space and activity centers.

9

SMART AND SPECIFIC

Goals, objectives, and KPIs

The basic concepts in measuring performance and accountability start with "SMART" goals, supporting objectives, and key performance indicators. These are heavily relied upon in the private sector, especially in larger corporations or those focused on metrics. But not every government agency has published goals and operational metrics that allow the public to see what the agency is focused on and the associated performance levels. Some are just so busy with daily activities or dealing with emergencies that they don't take the time to set these performance measures in place.

Almost every agency has a mission, vision, and values statement. These aspirational guidelines are important. However, without stronger agency alignment, leaders are highly unlikely to successfully deliver major initiatives or

SETTING PERFORMANCE TARGETS

GOALS (Year or multi-year)

Specific

Measurable

Achievable

Relevant

Time-based

OBJECTIVES (Monthly or semi-yearly)

A goal is aspirational, whereas an objective is operational and set to accomplish the goal. Objectives are more short-term, more specific, and much more clearly defined as actions or steps needed to be taken.

KPI'S (Daily or weekly)

Key Performance Indicators are metrics used to measure performance of ongoing processes in relation to strategic or tactical priorities. KPIs provide a snapshot and are typically measured against a range of criteria with desired minimum and maximum values or targets.

projects with predictability. The bureaucracy will continue to grow and expand and work in all different areas, many of which may be virtuous. But when people are working on items of personal interest or simply focused on the day's events, they may not be working on objectives to achieve an agency's ultimate goals. There's only so much time in the day, and employees may continue to expand activities and work on whatever they deem meritorious if they're not focused on established goals with adequate performance metrics. Consider the quote by Lewis Carroll, *"If you don't know where you are going, any road will get you there."* The inference is that one needs to know where an agency is going, which will then impact their pathway and what they do along that path – well-developed goals do precisely that.

The important thing to know when setting goals is to pursue both the priorities of the department and the policies of the elected officials and the CEO or city manager. The resulting goals should be specific, measurable, achievable, relevant, and time-based or "SMART." Then develop actionable objectives to meet each established SMART goal.

Then comes the crucially important key performance indicators or KPIs. These give a pulse on how your operation is doing in the near term or in "real time." A goal generally is measured after a longer period of time. In governments, usually, the evaluation occurs after a fiscal year or calendar year. Whereas key performance indicators measure what's happening all the time and are more operationally focused.

Suppose you're monitoring the turnaround time on permit processing for certain development categories. Your key performance indicators, with a set target for that function, will tell you how you're doing every day or week. You don't want to wait 12 months to find out you have poor performance in your customer service levels today and miss a chance to make course corrections to improve performance trends BEFORE customers start to complain.

Orange County Admin Building topping off event - Santa Ana, CA: Celebrating key milestones can positively impact goals.

10

POLITICS AND PARTNERSHIPS

P olitics, at its core, is the peaceful resolution of
conflict. Further, productive political relationships
for government agencies are important for a number
of reasons, including the fact that this can offer additional
opportunities for groundbreakings and ribbon-cuttings –
the importance of which was discussed in an earlier chapter.

Building positive political capital is important because,
inevitably, something's not going to go as planned. Perhaps
an audit's going to come back with a negative finding, or an
agency employee has a confrontational interaction with a
resident. Maybe a construction project doesn't end smoothly.

In the world of social media branding, press releases, and
quick news cycles, elected officials are routinely looking for
events to draw praise for what they're doing and what their
government agencies are accomplishing. A leader's thought
process should also include events that can be publicized
and trumpet the merits of an initiative.

Sometimes creativity is needed. In a previous job, a

Groundbreaking events: Celebrate the win and ensure speaking opportunities are included for local elected officials.

technology initiative introduced the capacity for online service requests via a virtual permitting software system. Because there was no shovel to put in the ground to do a groundbreaking, we had an event where a switch was thrown to turn on a large light bulb representing the computer system going live with this 24/7 customer service initiative. That was a novel way to bring energy, acknowledgment, and excitement to celebrate a key milestone of the initiative.

And then there are partnerships. Let's say you're a new leader trying to execute a challenging project. If you are not an agency like L.A. County, which is the largest county in the country, but you're next to L.A. County and have similar interests, you may be able to develop an important partnership. Your ability to achieve success is automatically going to be enhanced via that partnership for a legislative initiative or state or federal funding issue. Partnerships like this increase standing and capacities for advocacy well beyond what you would have had as only a smaller city or county. Always be on the lookout for common ground.

Finally, if targeted agencies do not initially see the advantage of partnering, your agency's elected officials can be requested to contact other elected officials to promote a spirit of cooperation.

Unions

Yes, unions were discussed in an earlier chapter, but that was in the context of employee relations and reforming the organizational culture. In this section, unions are positioned as a targeted potential political partner to get agency-wide efforts accomplished. Unions are important because they represent the workforce, but they also wield significant political capital with elected officials, with fire and police unions generally being the largest campaign contributors.

Accordingly, it's important to understand how unions interact with the elected bodies, as well as what their standing is in the community. Some unions may even represent multiple agencies in a certain geographic area. Changes that affect the workforce will almost always involve the union representatives, so it's important to understand the politics by partnering early on through meaningful engagements. Unions can then do their job in representing employee groups as you're trying to implement an initiative to improve your agency.

Joint powers authorities

Joint Powers Authorities or JPAs are a unique partnership mechanism that new leaders should understand because it involves the creation of a separate legal entity from two or more other government agencies. At some point, your agency may be considered for inclusion in a JPA. Additionally, this creates a potential new option for implementing a challenging initiative. If your agency does not have the authority to perform a certain action, but another local agency does have that authority, you can create a joint powers authority with combined authorities. This is a partnership that operates within your jurisdiction but as a separate legal entity. A joint powers authority can be structured to address elements of mutual concern to any of the formation agencies. It might be a taxation issue where one elected body doesn't support a tax for that certain initiative. However, another community might support it, so creating a JPA as a taxing mechanism might be effective because then the elected officials of your agency don't have to vote to raise taxes.

Another example is an infrastructure initiative, like a transit system that's going through multiple communities. The implementing agency could be a joint powers authority wherein each of the impacted cities within that area has representation on the board of that JPA. Associated project contracts and funding will be administered by the JPA on behalf of all the formation agencies.

Meteors give little warning: Positive relationships with elected officials and unions can help when disruptors hit.

CONCLUSION

There are more meteors in outer space than we could possibly count. Likewise, the local government workplaces in America also face numerous metaphoric meteors in these ever-changing times. As outlined in this book, meteors can appear in the form of natural disasters, cyber-attacks, an international military conflict, a global pandemic, continental supply chain disruption, and things we haven't yet imagined.

How about these meteors: What if Google or Amazon wants to locate in your community? How about the placement of a semiconductor factory? What about negotiating a development for a major sports facility or a spring training facility? We're just classifying those as meteors and things that do not occur in the regular course business.

The real issue here is that when those scenarios happen, inevitably, your attention will be diverted away from what you're trying to do on a daily basis in your agency. The majority of this book is about preparing your organization to be as efficient and effective as possible, so when that meteor creates disruption, your agency will be more likely to pass the preparedness test.

I call this preparation "managing for meteors," but

the primary essence is setting up your organization to be ready when that major disruptor eventually happens. If the meteor never comes, you will have at least established a more effective, efficient, and better prepared organization.

There is an interesting lyric in a Pearl Jam song where Eddie Vedder sings: "*I changed by not changing at all.*" This concept intrigued me because the world changed around the singer, which then actually changed his situation. I have told my teams that doing something or doing nothing is a conscious choice. And if you do nothing, that doesn't mean that ultimately nothing happens. The world continues to move ahead, which impacts the status quo and ultimately forces governments to adapt in areas with which they have traditionally struggled.

The meaning of public service in government

Growing up in the Midwest gave me the opportunity to see first-hand the benefits of a strong work ethic. Riding your bicycle down the road, you see farmers plowing fields or people going to work in the construction industry or driving to factories. New leaders in government must also work hard and be strategic to achieve a goal or overcome challenges – like Midwest snowstorms.

The role of government is to do for the people what they cannot do for themselves. Not everybody has a snowplow to clear their driveway. Not everybody can build a roadway or maintain a bridge or protect towns from flood events. The way the government helps to improve communities has always interested me, and it launched me on the path to decades of public service.

My aspiration for you, as a reader of this book, is that you will become better equipped to face the meteors that may affect your organization and the livelihood of the people you serve. Leaders in government should have a healthy respect for the responsibility given to them to serve those communities and encourage readiness as mitigation for eventual disruptors.

Shepherding public services that impact the quality of life for communities is both a high calling and a heightened duty. As Henry Ford's famous quote reminds us, "*You can't build a reputation on what you're going to do.*" Enhancing your organization's reputation and being as prepared as possible does not happen quickly or easily and can only be achieved through purposeful actions. The next steps are up to you.

ROAD MAP TO READINESS

1 Identify Issues and Define Plan Elements

- ☐ Conduct anonymous employee engagement surveys
- ☐ Review survey feedback versus industry trends and updated business practices - *Chapter 1*
- ☐ Engage leadership team to discuss survey evaluations and exchange ideas on improvement strategies - *Chapter 2*
- ☐ Evaluate organizational structures against efficiency metrics - *Chapter 3*
- ☐ Analyze operating budgets and trends to inform initial refinements through organizational structure efficiencies and zero-based budgeting strategies - *Chapter 4*
- ☐ Organize capital improvement project budgets through development of fiscally constrained and resource balanced, multi-year capital improvement programs - *Chapter 5*
- ☐ Review operational functions against industry best practices and develop initiatives to enhance efficiencies and effectiveness - *Chapter 6 & 7*
- ☐ Analyze services and assets for new or enhanced revenue initiatives to create budgetary flexibility - *Chapter 8*

2 Developing Next Steps and Goals

- ☐ Report out information to employees on proposed actions related to survey results and baseline efficiency enhancements or agency alignment with updated business practices
- ☐ Outline steps necessary to complete transition plans or new policy, practice, or procedure implementations
- ☐ Set SMART goals and supporting objectives to address each task or initiative and assign responsible person(s) - *Chapter 9*
- ☐ Determine deadlines for each of the targeted goals and objectives, including key milestones, and define the resources that will be needed

3 Measure Progress and Repeat Analyses

- ☐ Measure implementation progress against established metrics, and provide status updates to employees periodically or as available
- ☐ Report up to senior executives and elected officials and report out to the public on key goal achievements - *Chapter 10*
- ☐ Repeat the readiness process every 3 to 5 years

Made in the USA
Columbia, SC
29 January 2025

acbe612a-0885-4956-8251-ca1abefee1a3R02